Ingredients for a Happy Life ...

Tea, Cake, Meditation

by

Deborah Coote

Ingredients for a Happy Life ... Tea, Cake, Meditation
By Deborah Coote
ISBN 978-0-9563139-1-1

British Library Cataloguing in Publications Data.
A catalogue record for this book is available from the British Library.

Published by D.H. Lee, PO Box 209, Saffron Walden CB10 9DL

Book and cover design by Eleanor Tanner Design, Great Dunmow, Essex

Printed and bound in the UK by M & B Print Solutions Ltd., Great Dunmow, Essex

Additional copies

Available from the publisher, D.H. Lee, PO Box 209, Saffron Walden CB10 9DL

or **www.deborahcoote.com**

For Mum and Dad

who gave me everything

Acknowledgements

In this lifetime, I've had the good fortune to stand on the shoulders of spiritual giants. My deepest gratitude is to them.

Big love, too, for my dear friends, the Airy Fairies. This book is a tribute to your friendship, support and appreciation of tea, cake and the meditation mornings.

To Sandra Waller and Edwina Lark. How reassuring to know you are here to help me reach my potential this time around.

To Eleanor Tanner, whose creative ideas and inspiration have made this a very special project.

I would like to thank Susannah Whetstone, Marylyn Whaymand, Susie Keen and Sally Stephenson for their careful reading and invaluable suggestions.

Thank you also to Glenn Stephenson, Lesley Zorlakki, Susie and Sally for that brilliant Sunday afternoon brainstorming session that made everything crystal clear.

To my dear friend, Jane Gregory – thank you for the photographs, the brilliant blurb and for showing me how to appreciate afternoon tea!

A huge debt of gratitude goes to my Alexander and meditation students who teach me more than they realise.

Finally, to John. A thousand thanks for your patience, gentle nudging and encouragement.

About the author

Deborah was born in East London in 1964. Whilst working in banking, she took a part-time degree in French Studies at Birkbeck College, London, graduating in 1999, after which she went on to train as a teacher of The Alexander Technique.

She spends her time writing, teaching, lecturing and running inspirational and transformational workshops. Deborah also enjoys walking her dogs across the beautiful North West Essex countryside, where she lives with her husband.

Contents

Beginnings

Some years ago, a friend asked me to set up a meditation group. Over the years I'd attended various spiritual centres and retreats and had learnt how to meditate, the result of which then started to show up in my life in exciting ways. A new career teaching The Alexander Technique, a move to the countryside and the arrival of a moody Border Terrier called Bert had already meant many changes to my former, stressed-out way of city living.

So, with a deep breath and crossed fingers, I took my friend's advice and started an introductory meditation group which, over the last five years, has evolved into what is now affectionately known as the Airy Fairy Club. The original group of four has grown into fourteen committed and enthusiastic members, each practising meditation on their own as well as in the group – and have also become firm friends. In addition to this group, I run regular introductory and refresher workshops which are also gaining momentum, as many of the men and women who attend have become enthusiastic regulars!

Being part of a meditation group is fascinating and exciting as the energy and dynamics are constantly evolving. The combination of a quiet space in which to meditate, a cup of favourite tea (or coffee) with a slice of 'naughty-but-nice' cake, and time to chat, has helped many of us to become calmer, open minded and more adventurous in life.

To take a step into the unknown can be scary. There is insight and understanding of our true self the moment we make the decision to observe our thoughts, whether practising meditation individually or as part of a group. Order then begins to emerge.

Why not join the quiet revolution ... now *that* will be an experience!

With love and blessings,

Deborah Coote

Saffron Walden, Spring 2010

Inspiration

This book is a combination of things. It aims to inspire and enable you to set up your own individual and/or group meditation practice and, by doing so, the benefits of regular meditation will reveal themselves to you.

It attempts to strip away the misconception that meditation is mysterious or difficult. You'll discover that it's a practical and invaluable tool that helps your mind to stay calm, fresh and alert, allowing you to maintain a clear, balanced perception of life.

And finally, this book is a reminder of the importance of love and friendship experienced through sharing conversation, company, ideas or food, in an increasingly virtual and alienating world.

The book is in three parts and the approach is practical and realistic.

Part One explores all aspects of meditation, from help and advice in setting up an individual practice, to a summary of the benefits of regular meditation and any difficulties you may encounter.

Part Two describes how to go about setting up your own group, whether you host or facilitate, who to invite, and what time is best.

Part Three introduces the meditations and recipes. The chapters are divided into the four seasons, each season containing three different meditations, three recipes of my home baked cakes and inspiring words from very wise people.

You'll find a list of useful addresses in the back of the book, along with the titles of some inspirational books as well as an index.

Use this book in conjunction with the meditations on the companion CD, and you'll have everything you need to be on your way!

Part One

What is meditation?

Meditation explained

The dictionary definition of the word *meditation* is 'to empty or concentrate the mind in order to aid mental or spiritual development, contemplation and relaxation'. In Tibet, the word *meditation* means to become familiar. For most of us, however, the idea of being familiar with our minds seems a bit odd, because we think we know ourselves intimately, don't we? But if we stop and think about it, the reality is that most of our thoughts are firmly anchored in the past or future, or we go about our business on automatic pilot.

We get up, wash, dress, eat breakfast, drive to work, school or to the gym, and generally we have no idea how all these thousands of actions happened. Do you remember putting your socks or tights on this morning? Most of our thoughts and actions are habitual which means that we don't *need* to stop and think about them: they are below the level of our conscious awareness.

We are getting busier too. Stress, anxiety, fatigue, anger, insecurity, depression, low self esteem, not enough hours in the day ... these are familiar themes in contemporary life. We *escape* in many ways: by going on holiday; drinking; having love affairs; watching the telly; shopping; surfing the net. Distraction is a great way to avoid acknowledging our thoughts.

These diversions take us away from seeing the reality of our lives. Rarely do we share time, food or company in a way that used to be an everyday part of life. The word *companion* comes from the French word, *pain*, which means bread. Breaking bread together is rare, as are contemplative practices – remember how quiet Sundays used to be?

And yet, we've all experienced moments of complete attention: looking at a beautiful sunset or a work of art; listening to music; scoring a goal; walking in a forest; watching a child paint a picture. You'll probably agree that we'd all like to have these moments more often, and that's one of the reasons why I have written this book.

Meditation gives us a way of focusing the mind and of becoming aware of unhelpful thoughts thus allowing us to be sensitive to what is both inside and outside us at every instant.

Meditation increases our ability to be attentive. Only *we* can achieve this for ourselves. No one can do it for us.

Meditation frees the mind allowing it space to explore life with all its possibilities and potential, leading towards transformation as a natural outcome. Looked at from that perspective, why *wouldn't* you meditate!

The good news

Meditation is practical, useful and can be undertaken by anyone of any age, from all walks of life, or with the busiest or laziest minds. Let's face it, there are few of us who'd admit to owning a quiet mind, even those who engage in contemplative practices like T'ai Chi or spiritual Yoga. Meditation is about bringing the busy mind into a state of peace, understanding and clarity. It isn't about escaping or running away from life's difficulties, or controlling or subduing the mind, trying to turn negatives into positives. Rather, meditation enables us to gain insight into unhelpful thought patterns in a way that unifies our thinking, rather than dividing it. Regular practice raises our conscious awareness and, if we choose, it can transform the way we live.

For a while now, the West has been catching up with the East in its quest for spiritual insight, using science to uncover the mysteries of the mind. We are beginning to learn how the brain is configured and how all physical, mental and emotional responses are stored. In the same way that the unconscious habit of putting on our socks is 'hard-wired' into our brains' circuits, so too are responses that involve our emotions – anger, frustration, craving, desire – and like physical habits, these too, can be changed.

I used to think that watching TV soaps was

a great form of escape. Chatting to my mates at work about what we watched on the telly the previous evening was something to look forward to. Getting drunk occasionally was also a form of escape. Thinking back, most of my life was about what was next on the agenda: clothes, films and nights out. Living in the present would have seemed a bizarre concept back then. Focusing on my external appearance was really important as well, and I used to think that working out at the gym and eating organic broccoli was all I needed to stay healthy, completely ignoring my interior landscape.

So why didn't I feel right? Life had to change in some way. My first step was to enrol at the local Adult Community College, which ultimately led to my undertaking of a part-time degree. And then I booked on a meditation retreat for beginners which profoundly changed my life.

Learning to meditate can have profound changes on and in your life, too. By sitting quietly, you'll begin to see patterns of thoughts emerging and you'll learn to reduce the noise, the mental chatter that prevents you from knowing your true potential. You'll feel calmer, less tense, more alert and attentive to yourself, your surroundings and your family. And if you do become part of a meditation group, by meditating together and sharing your experiences, you may witness your friends change in similar and exciting ways.

The bad news

There is no such thing as a free lunch. Anything of value worth having can only come from commitment, and meditation is no exception.

You need to be disciplined, determined and patient. When establishing your own practice, there will be plenty of mornings when the alarm goes off, and rather than getting up fifteen minutes earlier, you'll want to turn over and go back to sleep. Or if it's before bedtime, the lure of a warm, comfy bed will be hard to ignore, especially in the cold, winter months.

Not having expectations is useful, too. There have been several occasions when people have said to me that they expected to have 'a big, life changing experience' when first meditating. Instead, all they felt was frustration at not being able to quieten their busy minds, or lessen the tension they noticed in their bodies.

Some people have written about these big experiences and, if we're not careful, we might also think this is what should happen to us. It's probably best to treat each meditation with what Suzuki Roshi calls 'beginner's mind', so that you don't fall into the trap of looking for the perfect meditation.

Slowly, however, you will find that by sitting quietly, even if only for a few minutes at first, you will become more aware of yourself, your surroundings, your actions and therefore, your life. The mystery of your mind will then begin to reveal itself.

Some common misconceptions about meditation

My mind is too busy – I'll never be able to control it

The busy or 'monkey mind' is something we suffer with and, if you are reading this book, you are clearly aware that your mind is distracted and you are ready to try something new to help calm it. We all have the potential to refine our thoughts. It just takes that first step.

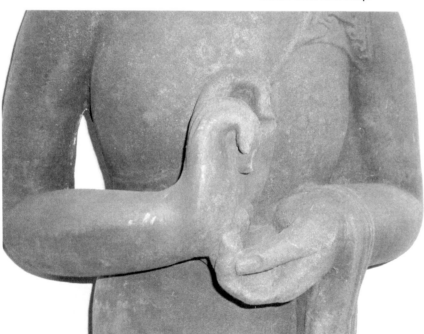

Don't be surprised when you begin to meditate just how busy your mind is. It's rather like shaking a jar of muddy water. At first it all seems a bit murky but given time, the mud settles and the waters clear.

I can't sit on the floor

A common image of a meditation posture is of someone sitting in a lotus position with ankles crossed, their hands outstretched and palms up. This is a shame, as I think it puts a lot of people off as they think it could be uncomfortable. It is for me. I sit either in a chair or on a meditation stool. All my workshops take place with the groups sitting on the sofa or on chairs and some people lie on the floor (more details about sitting positions are described on page 19). Sit on whatever you want, as long as you are warm and comfortable.

I'll have to give up drinking

If you want to become familiar with your mind and the type of thoughts you have, it makes sense to keep a clear head. After all, alcohol and drugs alter mind states, starving the brain of oxygen, so how can you raise your conscious awareness whilst under the influence? I enjoy a glass of wine occasionally, but the *need* to drink alcohol is no longer there. Since I began including meditation in my life, everything has changed, including my attitude to drink.

It's something only Tibetans do

There may still be the view that meditation only happens in the East. Since the sixties, however, eastern methods and techniques have been slowly absorbed into western culture. My generation is much more familiar with eastern practices so I tend to think this view is outdated. The Tibetans most certainly are well-known for meditation, but we are fast catching up. Scientific evidence emerging from ever more sophisticated imaging techniques verifies the benefits of meditation on mental and physical health and this knowledge is bringing a whole new audience to meditation.

The health benefits of regular meditation practice

This book is mainly for beginners in both individual and/or group meditation practice as well as refreshers.

At first it can seem bewildering to know how to choose from the thousands of different meditations available. In the spirit of simplicity, I've chosen some practical meditations that have particular benefits on our well-being.

Every thought, conscious or unconscious, is translated into a form of tension, particularly physical and emotional, and different types of meditation can have a direct impact on that. Using body awareness meditations, we learn how to recognise why and where tension is held. By redirecting our thoughts that allow us to let go, our bodies can start to work more efficiently and with more awareness. Intense body awareness gives us presence, keeping us in the here and now, whether we are sitting in meditation, or queuing at the supermarket. It is really useful.

Using the breath as a focus during a meditation activates parts of the nervous system that calm and sooth us, and can help to regulate heartbeat. There is scientific evidence that supports the view that meditation can help to lower blood pressure.

Visualisation and guided meditations (using images and pictures) help us to cultivate constructive and optimistic emotions, altering the way our bodies function. Using nature and the four seasons as a backdrop to these meditations can often remind us to re-connect with the glories of the natural world.

You'll find some analytical meditations, too (using insight and understanding). These alert us to feelings of self-centredness and ego, allowing compassion and empathy to rise to the surface.

Changing our mind about something can only really happen when we tune in to the types of thoughts we have and these are often unconstructive, judgemental and harmful. Like any physical habit mental thoughts and patterns can be changed with attention and watchfulness. A shift in perspective is then almost certainly going to follow.

How do I get started?

A few years ago on a retreat, I met a woman who had a husband and three young sons, and they lived in a small house. The woman told the group she used to meditate in her bathroom as it was the only room where she could find peace. She also used a bathroom cabinet as a small shrine!

Assuming you are going to begin to meditate on your own, your first consideration is where to do this. In an ideal situation, a dedicated meditation space could be created – somewhere for your chair/stool/cushions to be set out without having to put them away. Some people set up a shrine or altar on which they place flowers, photographs, icons, candles or other items of beauty or inspiration. If you like that idea, give it a try. One of the guys who attends my meditation workshops sits on a bench during his lunch break to meditate: others say they sometimes sit quietly for a few moments in their cars before driving off – any time, any place, anywhere – fantastic!

Find a space that is quiet with minimal distractions. Few of us are fortunate enough to live somewhere completely silent. Everyday noises like birdsong, traffic and people are constantly there but whilst we are going about our business, we may not notice them. During meditation the focus is on allowing distractions and noise to pass through your mind without disturbing you as after a while you'll become aware of your thoughts wherever you are. If you are brave enough to switch off your mobile, or unplug the landline, you won't be disappointed as there's nothing worse than your meditation being disturbed by the phone ringing.

Do I need a teacher?

When you are learning something new, it can be useful to find someone who has experience. For some of us, however, that's not possible or desirable. Why not be your own guru? Using this book in addition to the CD will get you started. You may wish to focus on just one or two of the meditations to begin with, until your mind becomes familiar with the new way of thinking. On the other hand, if you are drawn to certain meditations such as visualisation, start with those. Either way, regular practice is the key.

If you have experience in meditation and are contemplating setting up a group, for more information see Part Two: Setting Up Your Own Group.

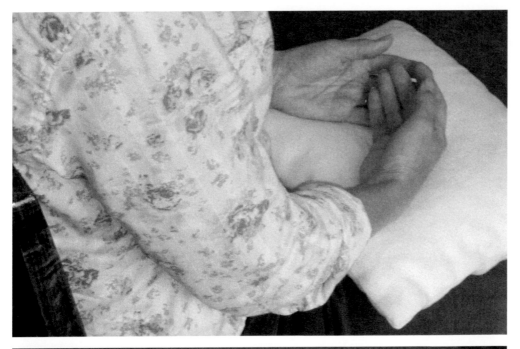

Sitting positions

My favourite meditation spot is in the living room, sitting on the sofa. If you prefer to sit on the floor, on a stool or on cushions, that's fine. We've all got a comfy chair, so head for that. In the colder months, I wrap a blanket around my shoulders or lap, and light a candle as it creates atmosphere. Sometimes I'll make a cup of tea before I start. Several of my students lie down in a position used in The Alexander Technique called 'semi-supine'. For some of the meditations this is especially helpful if you have a bad back or neck. For more information, see the Useful Information page at the back of this book. In the winter, my husband very kindly gets the wood burning stove going before heading off to work, so watching the flames is an inspiring start to my session. In the spring and summer months, I pull back the curtains to look out at the garden. It's important to be warm, so avoid sitting anywhere in a draft. The body cools down when we sit quietly, so remember to keep wrapped up if you feel the cold.

The Airy Fairy Club sessions take place in my living room, where we sit on a mixture of sofas, chairs and meditation stools.

Most of the meditations I attended in the earlier years involved sitting on cushions on the floor, but it was a difficult position to maintain without stiffness occurring, so I bought a stool which worked really well.

Comfort is the key here – resolving that will mean less distraction during your session.

If you experience pain or discomfort, the answer is to move. If the pain persists, you may need to seek professional help or have lessons in The Alexander Technique (see Index for more information). If you have a medical condition you are concerned about, it's always wise to check with your doctor before undertaking anything new or different and meditation is no exception. Also, if you find that meditation stirs up feelings or emotions that you feel you need to get help with, have a chat with a medical or healthcare professional.

The most important thing when sitting is to keep your spine straight. This may mean you need support in the form of cushions. The design of most meditation stools means that it is easier to maintain an upright position, even if you are a bit of a sloucher, so they can be useful. An upright spine means you'll be more alert in the meditation.

If you sit on a chair or a sofa, keep both feet in contact with the floor, allow your spine to be supported by the chair and rest your hands in your lap. Leave a gap between your arms and your ribs, so that your breathing isn't obstructed. These few adjustments have a direct impact on the amount of energy your body is using to keep you in position. A friend of mine thinks about her feet being really heavy as that keeps her physically grounded during the meditation. Another friend puts a cushion or book under her feet as her legs are on the short side. You'll be amazed at how these little things make a difference.

Some traditions of meditation ask you to keep your eyes half or fully open. I prefer to close mine. Why not experiment for yourself? If at any time you feel discomfort or anxiety and your eyes are closed, open them and come back to the room. It's also a good idea to re-focus your attention on your feet as that will ground you. You may see colours, swirls or patterns – this is normal, but again, if you are alarmed, just open your eyes.

What time is best?

The first group meditation class I attended when living in London was at 7pm. Although it was late, the difference in my energy by the end of the evening was amazing. After a while, morning meditation replaced the evening classes because it suited my temperament better as I am one of those really annoying, happy morning people! For those of you with children, mornings may be difficult. One of the group members does her meditation when she gets back from the school run. If you have children or go off to work, you'll find the best time to suit you.

Try to be as flexible as you can, because if you have a specific time set aside and

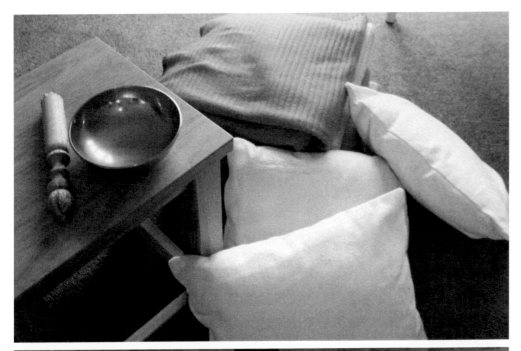

you can't make it on that occasion, you might not try again later. When I miss the morning session, it definitely affects my day. More recently, it's become a quest to find time to sit quietly, maybe at lunchtime, and not pick up the phone while eating my sandwich – now that's a miracle!

Be aware of the small voice in your head though – it will give you a hundred reasons why you shouldn't meditate. Some people call the voice their gremlin or the ego, and it is always fearful of us changing for the better. Whatever the voice is, give it a pat on the back and sit quietly anyway!

For how long should I meditate?

Anything between five and thirty minutes is a really good start. One minute can seem like an awfully long time when your mind is rolling along like a steam train!

If your mind wanders, a good tip is to return your focus through breathing or body awareness either of which will act as an anchor.

The other consideration is how much time you have for meditation. I recommend sitting quietly for five minutes if it's the only time that's available, as it's important to be consistent. If you are concerned about not knowing the time, place a small clock or watch in front of you so that you can glance at it. Some people set a timer when they start, but as time goes on, you'll get to know for how long you've been meditating.

It's worth saying that there is no such thing as a good or bad meditation. It is as it is, so whatever happens is fine. This is perhaps the one time in your day when you are consciously deciding not to compare – not to say to yourself, "well, yesterday's session was better/worse." This is very difficult as we unconsciously compare and judge ourselves all the time. Just do what you can. Be kind to yourself and know that you are taking the first steps towards change. Remember that old saying – Rome wasn't built in a day!

Typical difficulties

Mind-wandering

Don't be surprised, frustrated or angry if you notice your mind wandering. Busy mental chatter or 'monkey mind' is part of the human condition. It's said that the average person loses attention every six to ten seconds per minute! If that is true, what better reason for starting a meditation practice, as we need to become familiar with the mind in order to discover what type of thoughts we have. As we've already seen, mental chatter is just another habit which can be changed.

If your mind wanders, with patience, use the focus of your breath or body awareness to help bring it back. Remember, you are learning something new and you wouldn't expect to master the piano in a few weeks. Meditation is no different.

Fatigue or tiredness

When you close your eyes to meditate, you may find you feel sleepy. It could be that you are generally too busy, not stopping or resting until you fall into bed. When you make the effort to sit quietly, you may begin to notice how tired you are, and may need to take steps to remedy that.

Make sure you are sitting in a position which promotes an upright spine. You may find that the time of day you choose for meditation is a factor; if it's in the evening, it may be too close to your bed time. Try a different time of day. If the room is too dark, this can cause you to feel drowsy, so perhaps turn up the lighting to counteract this. Try keeping your eyes half open as this might help. You may also break the meditation into two parts, making each period a bit shorter. If the sleepiness is persistent after a few weeks, there could be other things going on in your life that may need looking into.

Physical discomfort

Getting comfortable is not as easy as you might imagine. Decide on the type of seat that suits you best, as aches and pains will distract you. Having said that, don't be alarmed if you notice some form of tension or strain. It may need your attention.

Part Two

Setting up a meditation group

The benefits of group meditation

Having spent time practising the meditations in this book or from the CD, or if you are already familiar with meditation, you may wish to set up your own group. One of the reasons the Airy Fairy Club is so great to be a part of is the sense of community and sharing. Nowadays, we are more cut off as individuals and miss the benefits that community and groups can bring – company, friendship, a sense of solidarity, sharing of ideas, support – all these things seem sadly lacking in our 'look after myself' society we now live in. It's common to spend so much time catching up with friends on social networking sites we have little time left for human contact. If we can't get online, we often experience a low level anxiety – a feeling we are missing out. On a more serious level this can lead to a real sense of alienation and loneliness.

Group meditation is a healthy antidote to that. It is also extremely powerful. When several minds focus on the same thing, such as health, love, happiness and peace, there is a ripple effect, spreading from the group into the wider atmosphere. Scientific studies have proven many times the beneficial changes that group meditation can bring – not just to the space in which you are meditating and the fact that you belong to a group, but to the wider community as well. (See Index for more information).

No matter what age you are, meditation will be of benefit. Some of the busiest people I've met are retired, packing in new experiences before they 'run out of time'. Experiences are about quality, not quantity. It is more important to become consciously aware of what you are doing so that you remember these experiences rather than them passing you by. If you keep busy because of fear – fear of running out of energy; fear of getting old; fear of stiffening up; fear of being alone or bored – certain meditations can help you to understand this pattern of thinking and, in time, change it. Meditating with friends of a similar age group will give you the opportunity to discuss these types of thoughts and beliefs, allowing for understanding and insight to emerge.

Some of the benefits of group meditation have already been described and belonging to the Airy Fairies has been hugely important in helping me grow as a human being. I know I speak for the group when I say how much we look forward to our Friday morning sessions, especially as we always have things to share, stories to tell and plenty of laughs. It truly is the highlight of my week!

Host or facilitator?

Hosting a group means providing a quiet room or space in which to gather. In the same way that book groups or coffee mornings are rotated, you may wish to take turns to host the sessions. You'll need to provide comfortable seats as it is really difficult to maintain focus if you are sitting on a fold-up chair. The number of people

you invite will therefore depend on things such as chair numbers and space. If you have cushions for resting hands on, great. If you don't have enough, your friends can bring their own, as well as a blanket, if needed.

If you are planning to use the CD, you'll require a CD player. Glasses for water, a small clock and a box of tissues are also useful. The most important thing is having a quiet room and noisy children, partners, dogs or neighbours may create tension in you and the group.

Facilitating a group is different. You may be happy to invite guests but not feel experienced enough to facilitate the sessions. If you have a friend who is calm, responsible, has done insightful work and is someone you trust, or you know someone who has practised regular meditation, you may want to invite her/him to facilitate your sessions, with you as the host. There are many possibilities, but the important thing is to have had some personal experience of meditation as the last thing you'd want is to feel out of your depth.

If at some point you'd like to become a facilitator and you'd like to find out more, sign up for one of my Setting Up Your Own Group workshops. For dates, visit: **www.deborahcoote.com/workshops**

The Friday Morning Meditation Session

The Airy Fairy Club meditation classes run on a four week on, four week off basis as it keeps the interest and enthusiasm going. Most people can't commit to a continuous, weekly class and I didn't want to commit myself to running too many sessions. There is quite a bit involved in setting up the house and I, too, like to remain enthusiastic about the classes. As we all have our own meditation practices, it isn't so important to meet more than we do. What's really great is that, after the four week break when we come back to the group, everyone is fresh and energetic. I also factor in a summer break – we don't usually get together in July and August due to holidays.

The group come to the house on a Friday morning, from 10am to 12pm, although we rarely finish at 12pm as we are so busy chinwagging! We are a combination of self-employed, retired, part-timers and parents, and Friday mornings work well. If you work full time, you may find the evening a good time to meet up, say from 7pm to 9pm, or maybe on a Saturday morning. If you are leading the sessions, choose a time that suits you best as most people who want to come along will fit in with you.

I set up the living room by putting out extra chairs, blankets and cushions. Candles are lit, and in the cold months, so is the wood-burning stove. You'll find that sitting for meditation cools down your internal heating system and you may find you've become cold, so keep your room warm and have some blankets handy. During the week I prepare a couple of meditations to read and bake a cake to share with the group. A tray of water, glasses and a box of tissues are always available in the room.

Certain types of music can enhance the atmosphere and whilst meditating on the wonders of the natural world, we might listen to the sounds of whales, the vibration of Tibetan chimes or Sufi music as this, in particular, makes for a wonderful 'colour and healing' meditation. Most of the time, however, the room is quiet. Occasionally, to mark the end of the meditation, I read from an inspirational book or poem.

The CD will be invaluable initially, as once you've chosen your meditations, you can sit with the group and follow it. You may want to start with a body awareness meditation to allow everyone to tune in. After you've started with that, you could follow with one of the visualisations or read from the book itself. The CD is there to get you used to the flow of a meditation, what speed to read at, where to pause and to allow you to relax.

One thing is certain – once you get started, you'll follow your own ideas and inspirations to make your group as uplifting and meaningful as you want it to be. This book is intended to spark interest by sharing my experiences and, in doing so, it may open a door into as yet unknown and exciting experiences of your own. Please remember though, it's not the only way.

Here is the programme for the Airy Fairy Group. Your meetings may happen in the evening or on the weekend, so please feel free to adapt the programme to suit you.

Meditation Session Programme

10.00am

The group arrive. Everyone gets set up with cushions, blankets etc. Mobiles are switched off, as there really is nothing more distracting than a dodgy ring tone! I also unplug the landline.

10.15am

We usually take it in turns to chat about our week – it's lovely to hear what everyone has been doing, especially when big events have been planned or have happened. The group talk about their own meditations of the previous week as, although we have a lot of fun, it is important not to lose sight of the purpose of getting together.

10.45am

Time for the first meditation to begin. To start the session, I ring the Tibetan singing bowl three times as this is an effective way

> *"As an older lady, I strongly recommend meditation as there is a tendency for retirees to feel anxious, thinking they have got to cram it all in. I am not so fearful now of running out of time, as I feel I have a coping mechanism for life."* **Margaret**

> *"After starting meditation classes my health improved greatly: here I could unburden the constant mental chatter that made my life very stressful."* **Benthe**

> *"On the days I meditate I am different: I am calmer, more centred and thus more able to cope. My vision is clearer and my approach to life more positive."* **Suzanne**

of marking the start and finish of the meditation. If you don't have a singing bowl, gently tapping a glass works well. The first meditation is generally a combination of body awareness and breathing. It's a great way of settling us all into the meditation and in a few minutes, everyone is quiet and alert. I then read the meditation, ring the bell at the end and allow time for everyone to come back to the group before inviting them to talk about their experiences.

11.00am

We spend a few minutes discussing individual experiences of the meditation. This is really useful and one of the reasons group meditation is so beneficial, as it becomes obvious that we share similar experiences, distractions, etc. Comments may range from, 'It took quite a while to quieten my thoughts' to, 'I managed to follow your voice throughout the whole meditation' to, 'I lost you at such and such a point, but saw wonderful colours and images' to, 'I didn't realise I was so tense/impatient/upset'.

11.10am

The second meditation begins. This will be either transformational, a visualisation, a healing meditation or a more detailed body awareness or breathing meditation. Like the first meditation, after it ends, we discuss what thoughts and experiences have come up, especially as these types of meditations often bring to the surface many different states of mind and emotional responses. For example, if we have focused our attention on a difficult situation or person, sometimes we may feel uncomfortable, angry or upset, so the discussion proves useful. Also, what tends to happen is that other members of the group may find similar things going on in themselves and, as a consequence, the discussion often leads to strategies and resources being shared ... a bit like mini brain-storming sessions! Sometimes, just before the end of the meditation, I read a poem or something uplifting before I ring the bell. Again, I give everyone an opportunity to talk about what has come up although sometimes there are no words to say, just smiles or snores!

11.30am – 12ish

Tea-time! This is a lovely end to the session because it is during this part of the morning that everyone is completely chilled out and there is a real energy in the room. Bertie the dog is allowed in at this point, causing mayhem! I make sure I have everyone's favourite tea, be it Earl Grey, Jasmine, Redbush, or good old builders to serve with the cake! We swap plans for the weekend, catch up on news and family, and also use the opportunity share information about various courses, classes and workshops that are going on. I aim to finish by 12pm but invariably no one wants to rush off!

Can I lead the sessions?

Why not? As it says in the Host/Facilitator section on page 26, if you have already been practising meditation for a while and have gone some way in working on yourself, there is no reason why you shouldn't have a go at leading the class. The thing is not to put yourself under pressure, as you may feel happier attending a group rather than facilitating it. You'll know if and when you're ready.

Some of the members in our group run their own separate meditation sessions in addition to coming to mine, but they are definitely good at inner management. Occasionally, I join other meditation classes as it's great for someone else to lead a group and I get to listen. Either way, you'll learn some great skills – organising sessions, becoming a good listener and facilitator, speaking and reading aloud, and honing your baking techniques!

Using the book and the CD

This book gives a fairly comprehensive account of the practicalities of meditation, so use it as a guide during your sessions. You can read from the book, play one of the meditations on the CD or use a mixture of both. Each meditation begins with a short introduction leading into the main section and ends with body awareness and breathing. When you hear the singing bowl ring three times it denotes the start and end of each meditation. A single ring of

the bowl indicates the end of that part of the meditation.

The CD has a selection of meditations taken directly from this book. The CD begins with a short introduction, followed by a *Body Awareness Meditation*. This can be listened to at various times of the day and not just with the group – perhaps before an event or a meeting, or before the family arrive or you might like to play it after they leave! You'll find several guided visualisation meditations such as *A New Morning*, *On the Beach*, *Autumn Leaves*, *A Winter's Walk*, which include body awareness and breathing. *A Wonderful Cup of Tea* and *Best Friends* are more analytical.

In fact, each meditation encompasses all aspects of what we require to change our minds but there may be occasions when you prefer more descriptive and creative meditations such as the visualisations, or prefer to become fully present and quiet, so using *Body Awareness*.

If the members of your group ask to copy the CD, I'd be really grateful if they'd buy a copy instead, as this whole project is self-funded, so I'd really appreciate your support.

If you buy six or more copies, the books and CDs are discounted. Visit:
www.deborahcoote.com/books/CDs

> *"During the meditation I feel calm, relaxed and at peace. I enjoy all of the morning, as it's great to spend time with nice people."* **Wendy**

> *"Meditation makes me slow down and take stock of what I am doing and what I am stressed about. It's nice to have the support of the group: we are all on the same level."* **Jacky**

Who should I invite to join my group?

My professional life involves running transformational groups and workshops, so people come mostly through recommendation or local advertising. The Airy Fairy Club began as a straightforward meditation class just like my other classes. It just so happened that after a while, we became good friends and the group expanded. In your case, you'll probably want to invite people you like spending time with, but it's worth mentioning to them beforehand that the session has a structure, otherwise you may spend so much time chatting there will be no time to meditate!

If you are the host/facilitator, you can ensure that everyone gets a chance to share their experiences and if someone is hogging the limelight, gently move them along. Try to avoid anyone offloading too many problems as this can have a less than beneficial effect on other group members. It may be an idea to start small, say with three or four friends, making the group manageable and work out how often you can meet. Not everyone in our group can make every Friday morning class but they always let me know. It may be worth checking the day before as invariably people cancel and you'll have spent time getting things ready. The advantage of having quite a big group is that when some

of the members can't come, we always have a good number.

If you are new to an area and you'd like to meet like-minded folk, ask around or put up a little card in the local shop window or library suggesting a meditation class. I've known a few people join classes in that way and, as a result, they've made new friends.

Have courage and give it a go. If it doesn't work out, you'll have learned a great deal and you'll probably continue with your own practice anyway. On the other hand, you may find that like our group, all sorts of interesting ideas and inspirations will emerge. Before you know it, you'll come up with a fun name like The Tree Huggers, or The Happy Clappy Group – these are some of our partners' nicknames for us! All your friends will want to join you and who knows what might happen next!

The cakes

Ah, the cakes! The cakes have become a bit of a thing now. I used to mention the type of cake I'd baked for the class before the meditations began, but it soon became distracting! One of my favourite things in life is to sit with a nice cup of tea and a home-made slice of cake, and I know the Airy Fairies feel the same. However, we've become so time poor that few of us have the time to sit quietly, let alone bake.

The cakes in the next section of this book are quick and easy to make. This method

"Now it is my best place to meditate and one of my happiest, most relaxed places to be." **Nicky**

"Since coming to the group I am less judgemental, more reflective, more in tune and calmer. I love the idea of meditation being practical and useful – really life-changing." **Marylyn**

Strange how a teapot can represent at the same time the comforts of solitude and the pleasure of company

Author Unknown

would probably be frowned upon by serious cooks but you can't be all things to all people. My week is busy, but I also like to spoil my friends, so I use mostly all-in-one methods which work for 90% of cakes I make. Sometimes my husband makes one for us which is a real treat because, as a former accountant, he likes to follow recipes to the number, which means his cakes turn out just right. He uses the food processor, which makes lighter sponges than my whisk does – I guess it's what you get used to. I've also included a couple of cake recipes for diabetic and vegan diets. Buy the best ingredients you can afford and remember to put lots of love into the baking!

You'll see below a list of equipment and utensils, most of which you'll have already. The recipes are adapted and are for well-known cakes as well as the more adventurous. They aren't perfect, but the Airy Fairies love them!

Whether you bake your own cake, buy one from a shop or pass around a packet of Custard Creams, it really doesn't matter. Whatever you decide, you'll find plenty to smile about just being with friends and sharing a lovely experience!

Bits and Bobs

Cake tins The better the quality, the longer they'll last and they won't let the cakes bake too quickly. Paper liners save on the

If man has no tea in him, he is incapable of understanding truth and beauty

Japanese proverb

Drinking a cup of tea will surely starve the apothecary

Chinese proverb

washing up, as do non-stick cake tins. The ones used here are 8inch round tins with removable bottoms or a 2lb loaf tin.

Mixing bowl My large Pyrex bowl was inherited from my dad. He inspired me to bake, as he used to put all the ingredients in one bowl, didn't use weighing scales and produced the most wonderful treats! Although I can't claim to have inherited his talents, the cakes produced from his bowl have done the trick ... thanks Dad!

Scales A good set of scales is essential, and for smaller measures, a set of measuring spoons is important. All spoonfuls should be level.

Sieves Apart from cake toppings, I no longer sieve flour or icing sugar (shock, horror!). If you like to sieve, a couple of different sizes are useful.

Spatula Plastic or flexible rubber spatulas are a must for scraping the bowl.

Electric whisk Although my husband uses the food processor when baking, I prefer the electric whisk (less washing up!). Hand whisking is tough on the shoulders, so try to avoid it!

Zester Needed for a couple of the recipes in this book but it won't be a disaster if you leave the zest bit out.

Paper liners and cases You can buy rolls of paper lining from any supermarket. Muffin cases are widely available, too.

Tea does our fancy aid,
Repress those vapours
which the head invade
And keeps that palace of
the soul serene

Edmund Waller ~ *Of Tea*

There is a great deal of
poetry and fine sentiment
in a chest of tea

Ralph Waldo Emerson ~
Letters and Social Aims

Part Three

Meditations
and
cake recipes

SPRING

Body awareness meditation

Body awareness

Focusing on our body gives us a straightforward and practical way into meditation. It is useful to begin all meditations with body awareness, as it allows the body to release tension as well as bringing about an increased sense of the self, wherever you are. Most people are so busy they don't notice the onset of tension, so becoming familiar with how your body is affected by your thoughts is really useful.

The meditation

Take some time to become quiet, allowing your body to relax and be comfortable. Let your eyes close. Feel the support of the chair or cushions behind you. Allow your mind to become still and quiet, connecting to the space and sounds around you. Bring your attention to your breath, noticing the rise and fall of your chest with each breath. Try not to be distracted by your thoughts. Allow any thoughts to drift through your mind, like clouds.

Become aware of your feet spreading out onto the earth beneath them. Notice the shape of your feet, letting them take up space on the floor. Allow your toes to soften and lengthen, and think of your feet widening. If you notice any tension in your feet, let it go, releasing it to the floor.

Now bring your attention to your legs. Feel the support of the chair beneath your legs, letting them become heavy, relaxed. Become aware of your knees, allowing any tension in your knees to release.

Notice your back. Feel the support of the chair against your back, allowing your spine to lengthen in an upwards direction, and let your back soften and widen. If you notice any tension across your back, think of it softening and releasing. As your back releases, tune in to your breath as it moves through your body.

Focus your attention on your neck. If you feel tension across your neck, think of it releasing, allowing your neck to become free and relaxed.

Become aware of your chest. Notice the rise and fall of each breath in your chest. If you feel tightness or tension around your rib cage, think of it releasing each time you breathe out. Take some time to stay with the spaciousness you feel in your chest and be aware of the spaciousness in your mind.

Notice your arms. Become aware of your wrists, elbows and shoulders, allowing your joints to soften and open, letting go of any tension. Let the muscles of your arms relax, allowing the weight of your arms to fall into the cushion on your lap.

Now become aware of your hands, feeling the cushion beneath them. Let your palms soften, and think of your fingers lengthening. As the tension in your hands begins to dissolve, become aware of the space and sounds around you, keeping your mind bright and clear.

Move your attention to your face. Beginning with your jaw, let go of any holding or tightening you may find there. Soften your cheeks, and rest your tongue in the bottom of your mouth. Now bring your attention to your eyes. Allow the muscles around your eyes to soften and relax, letting your eyes feel heavy. Notice your brow, and let the tension release. The smooth skin of your brow and face reflects the peace you feel on the inside.

As you feel your face relaxing, start to become aware of the rest of your body – your feet, legs, back, neck, shoulders, chest, arms, hands and face. Feel the whole of your body and mind expand into the space around you. You are quiet, calm, relaxed and present.

In your own time, bring your meditation to a close.

Nothing can bring you peace but yourself

Ralph Waldo Emerson

Rock cakes

As kids, my sisters and I used to visit our grandmother, nick-named 'The Cake Nan', once a month on a Sunday. At 5pm, she'd wheel in her trolley, filled to bursting with cakes of every description, and always with a plate of warm rock cakes.

Years later, I discovered how easy they are to bake and I've been baking them ever since. These rock cakes get a bit hard after a day but in our house, especially with Bertie the Border, they never last that long!

Cook 20 minutes   Serves 12

8oz / 225g self-raising flour
4oz / 110g butter or sunflower margarine
3oz / 85g caster sugar
5oz / 140g raisins and sultanas
2 eggs
A few tablespoons of milk

1 Preheat the oven to 190°C / 375°F / gas mark 5

2 Grease a bun tin or baking sheet

3 Rub the butter/margarine into the flour until it is crumble

4 Add the rest of the ingredients and mix with a spoon, leaving the mixture a bit stiff

5 Heap the mixture (about the size of a large egg) into the tins using two forks

6 Bake for 15 - 20 minutes until light brown

7 Transfer the cakes to the wire rack to cool

The new morning meditation

The new morning

Spring is a time for renewal, for growth and excitement. Nature is at its busiest, preparing the way for new life. As humans, we feel a shift in our internal landscape when spring arrives. It's a time when most of us are happy to be outdoors, enjoying the change in the atmosphere. This meditation celebrates the new season, helping us to appreciate the diversity and beauty of nature, and how much we are a part of it.

The meditation

Take some time to become quiet, allowing your body to relax and become comfortable. Gently close your eyes. Feel the support of the chair or cushions at your back. Let your feet spread out and take up space on the floor. Think of your spine lengthening in an upwards direction. Rest your hands in your lap, allowing your arms, neck and shoulders to soften and relax. Allow your mind to become still and quiet, connecting to the space and sounds around you. Bring your attention to your breath, noticing the movement of your breath throughout your body. Try not to be distracted by your thoughts. Allow any thoughts to drift through your mind, unobstructed.

It is a new day, the start of the new season. The long winter has finally, reluctantly, drawn to a close. Although still early in the morning, the sun is beginning to climb. It is warm. You walk up the lane, witnessing the last of the overnight frost melt in the unexpected warmth of the morning. As you walk on, a gentle breeze tickles your face. How exciting to feel the newness, the freshness of spring! A row of bright yellow daffodils stand to attention, trying to stay completely upright, but never quite managing to keep their heads balanced on top of their stems. It is such a cheerful sight. You feel your heart beat a little faster.

41

Pausing for a moment, you look upwards. The brilliant blue sky is peppered with small, white clouds, suspended in the air like cotton wool. Under your feet, you are aware of the damp, mossy leaves as you walk across the fresh, green fields. The birds sing wildly, full of hope and expectancy, busily building their nests, getting ready for the new arrivals. As you walk along the bank, you hear the soft sound of running water. A stream trickles below. You stop to look. And listen. Through the trees, shafts of sunlight create a dance upon the surface of the water. The stones glisten below.

In the distance, you hear the sound of church bells, so you turn and walk towards the chimes. Arriving at the church, you see a bench, so you go and sit for a while. All is quiet, peaceful. You feel the presence of all the souls who sat here before you, who once walked here and who are now resting peacefully. They are kept company by a wild fusion of spring colour: the dark purple of the grape hyacinth, the deep pink and creamy yellow primroses, the soft lilac crocus.

Suddenly, a small, light brown deer creeps out from behind a row of trees. You look at each other for a moment, observing each other's presence without fear or danger. You feel a tremendous sense of wonder at the sight of such a beautiful animal, each of you sharing a perfect moment. And you know that right here and now, all is well. The deer turns and goes on his way. You say goodbye and head home.

Gradually bring your attention back to your body. Notice your feet, legs, back, chest, arms, hands, face. Your body is relaxed and your mind is quiet. Start to become aware of the space and sounds around you.

In your own time, bring the meditation to a close.

> *All glory comes from*
> *daring to begin*
>
> **William Shakespeare**

Lemon drizzle loaf

This is another easy-peasy cake, but it's called a loaf as it's baked in a loaf tin. I always keep some greaseproof liners handy so I do not have to grease the tin. This cake works well with either butter or sunflower/soya margarine. It's also a particular favourite of one of the group, although the others never complain!

Cook 45 minutes   Serves 12

6oz / 170g self raising flour
6oz / 170g caster sugar
6oz / 170g butter or sunflower margarine
3 eggs
1 lemon
For the icing:
2oz / 55g icing sugar
Grated zest of one lemon

1 Preheat the oven to 180°C / 350°F / gas mark 4

2 Grease and line a loaf tin

3 Whisk all the ingredients including the juice and zest from half the lemon in the mixing bowl

4 Bake for 45 - 50 minutes in the centre of the oven

5 Leave to cool on a wire rack

For the icing:

1 Heat the other half of the lemon juice and the zest

2 Gradually mix the icing sugar with the hot lemon juice until it reaches a consistency that you can drizzle over the cake

Spring clean meditation

Spring clean

As human beings, our emotions cover the entire spectrum: from the brightness and light feelings of joy, happiness and bliss, to the darker, more complex emotions of anxiety, frustration, fear and anger. By combining the breath with brilliant light in this visualisation, we can purify the darker, unskilful thoughts, allowing a brighter and more natural energy to emerge, leaving us with a sense of peace and well-being.

The meditation

Take some time to settle into your chair or on your cushions. Gently close your eyes. Allow your body to relax, letting go of any tensions you may notice. Become aware of your feet, allowing them to spread out onto the ground, taking up space. Feel the support of the cushions or the chair at your back, allowing your spine to lengthen in an upwards direction. Rest your hands on your lap or cushion, feeling your arms, shoulders and neck relax. Your breath is quiet and calm, and your mind is beginning to expand as you tune in to the sounds and space around you. If thoughts arise, allow them to drift through your mind without becoming caught up or distracted by them.

Bring your attention to your breath. For a few moments, follow the gentle rise and fall of your chest with every out and in breath. Sense the gentle and calm movement of the breath in your body.

As you breathe out, visualise any dark emotions or feelings such as anxiety, frustration or anger leaving your body and mind as black smoke, dissolving into the space around you. With each out breath, the thick black smoke of anger, frustration, and anxiety is released from every cell in your body and mind. For a few moments, focus your attention on this black smoke being absorbed into the space around you.

As you breathe in, visualise a brilliant, white light full of health, vitality and well-being enter your body and mind. Feel every cell of your being absorb the powerful, healing white light, filling you with a healthy, vibrant energy. Each in breath brings lightness, peace, and wellness.

For a few moments, continue to breathe out your fears, anxieties and frustration as black smoke, and breathe in healing, purifying white light. With each new, full breath, know that you are healthy, happy and filled with a sense of peace, tranquillity and well-being.

Start to become aware of your feet beneath you, and your hands as they rest on your lap. Gradually notice the rest of your body: your legs, back, belly, arms, shoulders, neck and head. Extend your awareness to take in the space and sounds around you. Your mind is clear, bright and full of energy.

In your own time, bring your meditation to a close.

*Start by doing
what's necessary;
then do what's possible;
and suddenly you are
doing the impossible*

St Francis of Assisi

Apple and sultana muffins

These muffins are always a good bet as everyone in the AFC can eat them. Not great for Candida sufferers, though, but we don't have any of those in the group!

Cook 20 minutes   Serves 12

8oz / 225g eating apples, peeled and finely chopped
8oz / 225g rice flour
4oz / 110g sultanas
¼ teaspoon nutmeg
2 teaspoons baking powder
8fl oz / 240ml cup water
15ml / 1 tablespoon sunflower oil
1 egg, beaten

1 Preheat the oven to 200°C / 400°F / gas mark 6

2 Line the 12 muffin/bun tins with paper cases or grease the tin if you don't have cases

3 Mix all the ingredients except the apple in your mixing bowl but take care not to over mix

4 Add the apples and spoon mixture into the cases

5 Bake for 20 minutes in the centre of the oven

6 Leave on a wire rack to cool

Meditations
and
cake recipes

SUMMER

A wonderful cup of tea meditation

A wonderful cup of tea

Most of us would agree that it's the simplest things in life that bring contentment. Yet in reality, in trying to keep up with life's demands, we forget about the simple things. While we may not have the time for a Japanese tea ceremony, there is, nevertheless, something quite wonderful in taking time for tea. In this meditation, reflecting on the myriad causes and conditions that have to happen in order for us to enjoy our daily cup of tea can help us to appreciate the bigger picture.

The meditation

Take a few moments to become quiet, allowing your body to relax into your chair or cushions. Gently close your eyes. Keep your spine in an upright position, using the support of the chair behind you. Rest your hands in your lap, allowing your arms, neck and shoulders to relax. Let your feet spread out and take up space on the floor. Notice your breath moving through your body, becoming quiet and calm. Tune in to the space and sounds around you. Focus your attention on your mind, allowing space and lightness to appear. Let any thoughts pass through your mind without being distracted by them.

Bring to mind an image of you holding in your hands a cup of your favourite tea. For a few moments, contemplate how many people, events, conditions and causes are involved in getting your tea to the pot. Ponder the many different countries which produce your favourite tea: Redbush tea grown in the beautiful Western Cape of South Africa; green tea travelling from China's Hunan Province; Assam grown in lush, tropical conditions in India.

Reflect for a moment on the conditions required for tea to grow – the right amounts of sun, rain and temperature are essential, as is the outcome of the weather for the locals who rely on the income gained by selling tea. Think of the farmers that own the land, all those who plant, pick and dry the leaves and how the tea gets to the supermarket or shop; think of all those involved in the design, packaging, and transportation, and the staff in the shops that sell the tea to you.

Appreciate, too, the craftsmanship required to make your teapot, cup and spoon – the clay, the potter, the paint, and the painter. And in making the tea, there is the need for water, the fuel we use to boil it and how we find the means to pay for it.

Finally, as you visualise yourself taking a sip from your cup, reflect upon everything that had to happen to *you* in order for you to have the insight to appreciate such a simple, comforting and familiar thing like drinking tea, that could so easily be taken for granted.

By looking with a big mind at something we don't really think deeply about, we can begin to appreciate how much we rely upon nature and the hard work of others to provide us with our lovely, refreshing cup of tea. Knowing this helps us to recognise how complex and interconnected all life is, and how we, too, have an important part to play. The next time you put the kettle on, have a real sense of gratitude for the marvels involved!

Start to become aware of your feet beneath you, and your hands as they rest on your lap. Notice your breathing, feeling it move calmly through your body. Gradually notice the rest of your body – your legs, back, belly, arms, shoulders, neck and head. Extend your awareness to take in the space and sounds around you. Your mind is clear, bright and full of energy.

In your own time, bring your meditation to a close.

Tea is only this –

First you boil the water,

Then you soak the tea,

Then you drink it.

That is all you

need to know.

Rikyu

Victoria sponge

This cake is one that my husband or I always bake if we want a 'quick cake fix'. You know those moments when you're sitting watching the telly and fancy a cake but you have nothing in the kitchen and the shops have closed? Well, we'll bake one of these because they are simple, quick and delicious, and we've usually got the ingredients in the cupboard.

Cook 25 minutes   Serves 8 - 12

6oz / 170g self-raising flour
6oz / 170g butter (soft) or sunflower margarine
6oz / 170g caster sugar
3 eggs
2 drops of vanilla essence
2 drops of warm water

Butter cream filling (optional):
2oz / 55g butter whisked with **2oz / 55g** icing sugar

Raspberry or strawberry jam filling with icing sugar for topping (optional)

1 Preheat oven to 190°C / 375°F / gas mark 5
2 Grease two 8inch sandwich tins and line with greaseproof paper
3 Put the flour, butter, sugar, eggs and vanilla essence into the bowl and whisk until light and creamy
4 Divide the mixture between the sandwich tins
5 Bake in the centre of the oven for 20 - 25 minutes or until springy to the touch
6 Allow cakes to cool for 5 minutes and turn out onto a wire rack
7 When the cakes are cool, peel off greaseproof paper
8 Spread the jam on bottom side of one of the sponges (and the butter cream filling on the other) and sandwich together
9 Sprinkle the icing sugar over the top with a small sieve

Healing light meditation

Healing light

When we feel unwell, fatigued, anxious or downhearted, it's amazing how light lifts our spirits, helping us to feel better. SAD (Seasonal Affective Disorder) is becoming a common complaint these days, as many of us work inside, under artificial lighting. Even when at home, we can become so involved with tasks that we don't even take a break to walk outside, thus depriving our bodies of much needed vitamins and light. This meditation can help to remedy the effects of natural light deficiency. By visualising light in our minds and bodies, we create the conditions for health and well-being, wherever we happen to be.

The meditation

Take some time to become quiet and still. Feel your body begin to relax into the chair or on the cushion, letting go of any tensions you may notice. Gently close your eyes. Become aware of your feet beneath you, and your hands as they rest on your lap. Extend your awareness to take in the space and sounds around you. Follow the movement of your breath in your body, sensing the rise and fall of your chest with each breath. As you become quiet and calm, your mind begins to clear itself of thoughts, allowing a space and energy to emerge.

Visualise in the space above your head a disc or circle of brilliant, white light. You can feel the vibration of this light, pulsating in the space above your head. Begin to feel this light move down through the top of your head, travelling down into your body, spreading out into every cell until you feel the whole of your physical self filled with light.

As the beautiful, powerful, white healing light is absorbed into every cell of your being, feel yourself become weightless – your organs, nerves, blood, bones, muscles and skin are transformed by this powerful, healing energy. Have a sense of your body becoming a field of light, rejuvenating the whole of your body and mind as it vibrates. Know that all your pain, illness, fatigue and dark emotions have vanished, leaving you with a profound sense of peace and tranquillity. Your body feels alive, strong and healthy. Your mind is alert, bright and spacious.

Stay with these sensations for a few moments, enjoying the feeling of complete health and well-being. Notice your breath as it moves through your body. Notice your body feeling peaceful and serene. Notice your mind feeling expansive and full of energy.

Gradually become aware of your feet beneath you, and of the space and sounds around you. Your breath is quiet and calm, and your mind is bright and clear. Have a sense of gratitude for the benefits that this meditation has brought you.

In your own time, bring your meditation to a close.

The real voyage

of discovery consists

not in seeking

new landscapes,

but in having new eyes

Marcel Proust

Banana and apricot loaf

I sometimes make this loaf with a combination of rice and spelt flour, or I use dates instead of apricots. Either way, it is super quick and probably one of the healthiest cakes in this book (an oxymoron, if ever there was one!).

Cook 50 minutes   Serves 8 - 10

8oz / 225g self raising flour
4oz / 110g granulated sugar
3oz / 85g soft butter or margarine
1 large egg
4 ripe bananas
4oz / 110g chopped apricots

1 Preheat the oven to 180°C / 350°F / gas mark 4

2 Grease and line a 2lb loaf tin

3 Put all the ingredients except the fruit into the large mixing bowl and whisk until combined

4 Mash the ripe bananas and add to the mixture along with the chopped apricots

5 Pour into the loaf tin and bake in the centre of the oven for 50 minutes, or until the loaf is golden

6 Leave to cool for 10 minutes

7 Turn out onto a wire rack

On the beach meditation

On the beach

The expression to 'come back to our senses' is a clue to how much of life is spent living unconsciously. Our mind is usually somewhere in the past or future – rarely resting in the present. In this meditation, the focus is on using the senses in a way that increases awareness of our inner and outer landscape. In time, we are better able to stay 'awake' and connected, wherever we are.

The meditation

Take some time to settle into your chair or on your cushions. Allow your body to relax, letting go of any tensions you may notice. Become aware of your feet taking up space on the ground beneath you. Rest your hands on your lap or cushion. Your breath is quiet and calm, and you are aware of the space and sounds around you. If thoughts arise, allow them to drift through your mind without becoming caught up or distracted by them.

You are walking barefoot along a beautiful, sandy beach. The late morning sun is warm, and the beach is empty. As you walk, you feel the softness and warmth of the sand shift under your feet. You notice the texture of the sand change, becoming slightly cooler and rougher as you approach the water's edge. You feel the warmth of the sun upon your arms while a very light breeze blows your hair.

Pausing for a moment to take in the view, you are amazed at how the beach stretches out as far as the eye can see. The sky, a deep blue canopy, stretches out above with only a few wisps of lazy white clouds dotted around. As you listen to the waves gently lapping the shore, you notice how your breath begins to match the ebb and flow of the water. Like the never ending movement of the waves, so your breath is in constant movement, supporting your life with each full breath. You smell the fresh, salty air, allowing it to fill your body, and as you look up, you hear the call of a lone seagull as he swoops and darts in the air, finally diving into the shimmering sea.

Looking down for a moment, your eyes are drawn to a small, white, glistening pebble embedded in the sand beside you. You pick it up, brushing off the wet sand, and hold it in your hand, feeling its smooth texture, admiring its shape and colour.

And as you stand there, you are overwhelmed with a sense of peace, aliveness, of knowing you are connected through your senses to the splendour around you. You say a silent thank you for this glorious moment, before walking on.

Start to become aware of your feet beneath you, and your hands as they rest on your lap. Your breathing is calm, relaxed and steady. Gradually notice the rest of your body: your legs, back, belly, arms, shoulders, neck and head. Extend your awareness to take in the space and sounds around you. Your mind is clear, bright and full of energy.

In your own time, bring your meditation to a close.

Do not go where

the path may lead,

go instead where

there is no path and

leave a trail

Ralph Waldo Emerson

Lemon and poppy seed cake

This cake used to be my favourite whenever I saw it in a cafe, as it seemed really posh. It felt strange but adventurous to be eating poppy seeds. Years later, I found out it wasn't that difficult to bake, so for a long while, any visitor who came to the house was offered a slice.

Cook 1 hour   Serves 8 - 10

8oz / 225g plain flour
8oz / 225g sugar
4oz / 110g butter / margarine
4 eggs
2 teaspoons baking powder
5fl oz / 150ml milk
3oz / 85g poppy seeds
Finely grated zest of **2** lemons
The glaze:
Lemon juice from the **2** lemons combined with **2oz / 55g** granulated sugar

1 Preheat the oven to 170°C / 325°F / gas mark 3
2 Grease and line a deep cake tin
3 Place all the ingredients in the mixing bowl and whisk
4 Pour into the cake tin and bake in the centre of the oven for 1 hour or until the top springs back when pressed
5 Turn out onto a wire rack to cool
The glaze:
1 Combine the lemon juice and sugar in a small saucepan, bring to the boil and then simmer for 5 minutes
2 Using a skewer, prick holes in the top of the cake and then pour over the glaze

61

Meditations
and
cake recipes

AUTUMN

Autumn leaves meditation

Autumn leaves

Autumn is the season for reflection. It's a time when nature's pulse slows down, allowing a pause, before winter hibernation. Autumn colours are at their boldest and most brilliant, a last chance to shine for another year. In this meditation we reflect on how the passing of time brings us wisdom, as it is through experience that we choose how we live.

The meditation

Take a few moments to become quiet, allowing your body to relax into your chair or cushions, supporting your spine in an upright position. Gently close your eyes. Rest your hands in your lap, letting the weight of your arms fall into the cushion. Feel your feet spread out, taking up space on the floor. Become aware of the movement of your breath as it moves though your body, sensing the rise and fall of each breath in your chest. Bring your attention to your mind, feeling it expand as your thoughts dissolve into the space. Tune in to the space and sounds around you.

Visualise yourself walking along a country lane, lined with trees. The weather is beginning to show signs of cold, but there remains a hint of warmth on this autumnal afternoon. The sky above you is at its brightest, just before the early sun sets for the day. Jostling for space along the lane are mosaics of leaves, their sole purpose to catch your eye as you walk. Brilliant burgundies, crimsons and reds contrast with sparkling emeralds, limes and yellows, glorious in their diversity. You pick up a few, feel their texture, and put them in your pocket.

Walking across the fields, you notice the changing landscape. Trees that, until a few weeks ago, were laden with fullness and colour, now bare their spindly branches. The fruit on the blackberry bush is sparse. A few birds pick the last of the season's berries.

You head towards your favourite bench and sit down. And as you rest, you reflect on the passing year, reviewing the experiences you've had. You recall a previous situation in which you were unhappy and how, at the time, you wanted it to be over. Now, those unhappy feelings have passed, like the seasons, and you have learned much from this experience.

You now recall a recent time when you were full of joy, feeling on top of the world, full of energy and vitality, and how you didn't want this time in your life to end. You realise in this moment how feelings and emotions are fleeting, constantly changing. Everything passes with time. There is no point in trying to hold on to or recapture the past. You resolve to learn from these experiences, welcoming joy into your life but not being fearful of challenging times. With this new insight, you rise from the bench, taking a last look around you, and walk home.

Start to become aware of your body – your feet beneath you, your hands in your lap, your spine supported by the chair. Notice the movement of your breath in your body, and the space and sounds around you. Your mind is bright, alert and full of energy.

In your own time, bring your meditation to a close.

Nature herself makes

the wise man rich

Cicero

Choc brownies

These lovely little cakes are always a favourite — it's amazing how the word 'chocolate' can raise a smile! I sometimes use rice flour as one of the group members has a wheat allergy. It's best to let the cakes cool for a while as mine always break up if I get them out of the tin too soon.

Cook 35 minutes   Serves 12 - 14

4oz / 110g plain flour
4oz / 110g good quality dark cooking chocolate
8oz / 225g caster sugar
4oz / 110g butter
2 eggs (Use 3 eggs if using rice flour)
½ teaspoon baking powder (Use a full teaspoon with rice flour)
4oz / 110g chopped walnuts
Pinch of salt

1 Preheat oven to 180°C / 350°F / gas mark 4

2 Grease and line a shallow square tin

3 Melt the chocolate and butter on a low heat, either in a bowl over a saucepan of hot water, or in a small pan.

4 Put the rest of the ingredients in a bowl, except for the walnuts, adding the melted chocolate and butter, and mix well with a spoon

5 Add the chopped walnuts

6 Pour into the tin and bake in the centre of the oven for 30 - 35 minutes

7 After cooling for 10 minutes, transfer onto a wire rack to cool

8 Cut into squares

Best friend meditation

Best friend

Although we all share the same wish to be happy, it can seem that happiness is something that other people experience. Often, we find it hard to feel good about ourselves, which makes happiness seem ever more elusive. The focus of this meditation is to generate feelings of love and friendliness for ourselves, allowing happiness to emerge. By bringing to mind the qualities of someone we love and admire, and directing them towards ourselves, we can learn to appreciate our gifts and talents, becoming our own 'best friend'.

The meditation

Take a few moments to settle down and become still. Feel your body begin to relax into the chair or on the cushion, letting go of any tensions you may notice, and let your eyes close. Allow your spine to lengthen in an upwards direction. Become aware of your feet beneath you, and your hands as they rest on your lap. Notice your breath as it moves through your body. Extend your awareness to take in the space and sounds around you. Your breath is quiet and calm and your mind is clear, bright and full of energy.

Before beginning, take a few moments to bring to mind the image of someone you like, love or admire. It could be a friend, a member of your family, someone you work or spend time with. Allow your feelings for this person to arise. What qualities does this person have that you admire? They may include kindness, patience, and compassion. This person may be attentive, generous, good-natured. Notice how easy it is to want this person to be happy. Bring to mind a recent situation or time you spent with this person. Recall how wonderful it felt to be in their company. As you think about this person, be aware of the movement of your breath in your body. Be aware too, of feeling relaxed, calm and still. You may experience these feelings as a light or warmth around your heart. Allow this light to fill your heart as you think of this person.

And now, begin by wishing yourself peace and happiness. Generate a sense of acceptance of yourself, and allow the feelings of warmth in your heart for your friend to include you. As you reflect on your own life, know that like others, you wish to be happy and like others, you wish to be well. Feel the warm, healing energy from your heart move around your body, filling every cell with happiness, well-being and peace. Say to yourself,

"I am happy. I am well. I feel peaceful."

Make a commitment to spend some time focusing on your qualities, gifts and talents, generating warmth, acceptance and love for yourself. Start to pay attention to the good things about yourself, and in time, you will feel as cherished as those you love.

Gradually become aware of your feet beneath you, and of the space and sounds around you. Your breath is quiet and calm, and your mind is bright and clear.

In your own time, bring your meditation to a close.

And in the sweetness

of friendship let there be

laughter and the sharing

of pleasures.

For in the dew of little things

the heart finds its morning

and is refreshed

Khalil Gibran

cranberry, blueberry and raisin cake

Using cranberries and blueberries makes a change from sultanas and dates but any combination of dried fruit will work perfectly well.

Cook 1¼ hours   Serves 8 - 10

12oz / 340g self raising flour
6oz / 170g butter or sunflower margarine
6oz / 170g caster sugar
3 eggs
½ **teaspoon** mixed spice
5fl oz / 150ml milk
4oz / 110g cranberries
2oz / 55g blueberries
2oz / 55g raisins

1 Preheat oven to 180°C / 350°F / gas mark 4

2 Grease and line a deep cake tin

3 Place all ingredients except the fruit in the mixing bowl and whisk

4 Add the fruit and stir in with a spoon

5 Pour into the cake tin and bake in the centre of the oven for 1¼ hours or until the top springs back when pressed gently

6 Turn out onto the wire rack to cool

Inner strength meditation

Inner strength

Nature has a way of helping us to help ourselves. When we look at a tree, it brings to mind attributes like upright, strong, resilient, wise, great, powerful, firm, flexible, sturdy, How many of these characteristics can we apply to ourselves? Bringing to mind a natural, beautiful object such as a tree can help us to apply these qualities to ourselves, helping us to be well in times of illness, anxiety or tension.

The meditation

Take some time to settle and become quiet. Allow your body to begin to relax into the chair, or on the cushion, letting go of any tensions you may notice. Let your eyes close. Keep your spine in an upright position, lengthening into the space above your head. Become aware of your feet beneath you, letting them spread out onto the earth beneath them. Allow your hands to rest on your lap, supported by the cushion. Follow the movement of your breath in your body, sensing the rise and fall of your chest with each breath. Extend your awareness to take in the space and sounds around you, becoming quiet and calm. Your mind is bright and clear, full of space and energy.

Bring to your mind the image of a tree. Think of the roots of the tree, spreading down deeply into the earth and gradually moving outwards. Think of the trunk of the tree reaching upwards into the sky. See yourself sitting with your back lengthening and widening against the great tree. Have a sense of your spine connecting with the trunk, absorbing its power. As you absorb the feelings of strength, become aware of the movement of your breath in your body.

Have a sense of the tree's age and wisdom. Reflect on the passing scenes the tree has witnessed and how, many times over, it has experienced the whisper of the wind, the sun's smile, the bite of frost, seasons passing, the birth and death of birds, insects and animals. And yet, the tree maintains its strength, stillness and composure.

For a few moments, reflect on the passage of time in your own life and how you are here, now, and like the great tree, still growing in wisdom and strength. Think of yourself as being flexible, stable, resilient, able to withstand the unpredictability of life with grace and courage. Make a commitment to yourself to take the time to appreciate the beauty and wisdom of your own true nature.

Gradually let your awareness expand to take in the whole of your body. Become aware of your feet beneath you, feeling connected to the earth, like the roots of the tree. Begin to take in the space and sounds around you. Your breath is quiet and calm, and your mind is bright and clear.

In your own time, bring your meditation to a close.

Energy and persistence

conquer all things

Benjamin Franklin

Coconut and jam slices

Coconut was all but a distant memory until I began thinking about different types of cakes to give to the group. This basic sponge with desiccated coconut added in, topped with strawberry or raspberry jam and more coconut sprinkled on top, reminded me of a type of pudding we used to eat at primary school but without the custard. Thank you to the brilliant cooks at Seabright Primary School for making school dinners such a treat!

Cook 40 - 50 minutes   Serves 10 - 12

5oz / 140g self-raising flour
6oz / 170g caster sugar
6oz / 170g butter or sunflower margarine
2oz / 55g desiccated coconut with extra to sprinkle on top
3 eggs
Strawberry or raspberry jam

1 Preheat the oven to 180°C / 350°F / gas mark 4

2 Grease and line a loaf tin

3 Whisk all the ingredients, including the dessicated coconut, in a mixing bowl

4 Bake for 45 - 50 minutes in the centre of the oven

5 Leave to cool on a wire rack

6 When the sponge has cooled down, spread a thick layer of jam over the top and sprinkle coconut on top of the jam

Meditations
and
cake recipes

WINTER

A winter's walk meditation

A winter's walk

During the long winter months, we can get cocooned indoors keeping warm, caught up with distractions and reluctant to venture outside unless it's necessary. We may feel a bit down at this time of the year, particularly if snow has kept us from going about our daily business. And yet, every season brings its own beauty, mystery and wonder, awakening in us a sense of exploration and adventure if we are brave enough to venture out. Looking at familiar scenery throughout the seasons with fresh eyes, can help us to appreciate the landscape in which we live and not feel trapped by it.

The meditation

Take a few moments to become quiet, allowing your body to relax into your chair and your spine to be supported by the cushions or chair at your back. Gently close your eyes. Rest your hands in your lap, and let your feet spread out and take up space on the floor. Become aware of your breathing, the gentle rise and fall of your chest with each full breath. Bring your attention to your mind, creating space and expanse. Let any thoughts pass through your mind without being distracted by them.

It's a cold winter's day and you decide to go for a walk. Snow has been falling silently overnight, covering the fields with a thick white blanket, as yet untouched by human footsteps. As you walk along the wintry path, you take care to step lightly, staying balanced on the slippery ground. This is a familiar route, one you have walked regularly, so you settle into a confidence that comes with knowing where you are heading.

Reaching the footpath, you observe the vast space around you. You are completely alone in this cold and snowy setting, and the frozen earth beneath your feet crunches and cracks as you cross the field. Each step breaks the silence of the morning. You enjoy the sense of freedom, of being outside in the space, wrapped up warmly against the cold day, breathing in the crisp, icy air.

You stop for a moment, tuning in to the silence of the winter landscape, knowing that tomorrow nature will be different again, constantly changing, full of surprises, like life. You tune into your senses: feeling the cold tingling in your fingertips; hearing the faint trickle of a stream running alongside its frozen banks; smelling wood smoke from the chimney of a nearby cottage.

These thoughts bring you back to your body as you realise you've walked full circle and you are just a few footsteps from the warmth of home. You feel alive, expanded, connected and happy to have taken the time to admire the wonders of the winter walk.

Start to become aware of your body – your feet beneath you, your hands in your lap, your spine supported by the chair. Notice the movement of your breath in your body, and the space and sounds around you. Your mind is bright, alert and full of energy.

In your own time, bring your meditation to a close.

Appreciation

is a wonderful thing:

it makes what is excellent

in others belong

to us as well

Voltaire

choc, walnut and blackberry vegan loaf

One of the really fantastic things about living in the countryside is being surrounded by fields lined with blackberry bushes. Every September, blackberry picking is the name of the game. One of my 'peak' experiences was picking berries as the sun was setting over the fields – magic! This vegan cake is delicious with blackberries or, if not in season, raisins.

Cook 50 minutes   Serves 10 - 12

6oz / 170g self raising flour
5oz / 140g caster sugar
3fl oz / 75ml vegetable or sunflower oil
3oz / 85g blackberries (or raisins)
2oz / 55g cocoa powder
2oz / 55g chopped walnuts
¾ **teaspoon** bicarbonate of soda
½ **teaspoon** baking powder
1 teaspoon vinegar
8fl oz / 240ml soya milk
½ **teaspoon** vanilla essence
¼ **teaspoon** salt

1 Preheat oven to 180°C / 350°F / gas mark 4
2 Grease and line (or use liner) 8 inch deep cake or loaf tin
3 Whisk all the ingredients except the blackberries and walnuts in the mixing bowl
4 Add and mix in the berries and walnuts
5 Bake in the centre of the oven for 50 minutes or until the top springs back
6 Leave to cool on a wire rack

Balance and poise meditation

Balance and poise

Equanimity means to have an evenness, composure and poise. A balanced, even mind, allows us to not be troubled by thoughts and not react to our reactions, maintaining a clear perception of things and events as they are. Using this meditation to focus on a balanced state of mind during or after times of stress or anxiety, can dampen the stress-response system, and help to break habitual reactions and feelings.

The meditation

Take some time to become quiet, allowing your body to relax and become comfortable. Let your eyes close. Feel the support of the chair or cushions behind you, allowing your spine to stay upright. Let your mind become still, quiet, connecting to the space and sounds around you. Bring your attention to your breath, noticing the rise and fall of your chest with each breath. Try not to be distracted by your thoughts, allowing them to drift through your mind, unobstructed. Feel your mind become spacious, bright and clear.

Bring to mind a situation, event or a time during which you felt stressed or anxious. Remind yourself of how you felt – were you angry, impatient, flustered? Can you recall any physical reactions surfacing during this situation – were your neck or hands tense, could you feel your heart beating faster than usual? Relive this experience for a few moments, paying particular attention to your heartbeat, breathing, hands and neck.

Allow this image to fade from your mind and come back to your body, noticing your feet on the floor, your hands on your lap, and your breath moving through your body. Stay with the movement of your breath for a few moments. Notice the rise and fall of your chest with each breath.

Now refocus your attention on this situation but this time, visualise a space around the scene, as if were happening on a stage with you as an onlooker, an observer, feeling calm, balanced and poised. Become aware of any feelings or emotions that may arise whilst thinking about this situation or event but try and retain an awareness of your breath, keeping it steady.

Maintain an awareness of your hands, keeping them soft and open and ask for softness around your neck. You no longer feel stress or anxiety, just a deep sense of peace and tranquillity as the image fades from your mind.

Bring your attention back to your body. Notice your feet, legs, back, chest, arms, hands and face. Check that your body feels relaxed, and your breathing is calm and regular. Start to become aware of the space and sounds around you.

In your own time, bring your meditation to a close.

> *A journey*
>
> *of a thousand miles*
>
> *begins with a single step*
>
> **Lao Tzu**

carrot cake

My husband usually bakes this cake and everyone raves about it. He uses the food processor because like most boys, he just loves the whole gadget thing. This cake works just as well being mixed in a large bowl (and there is less washing up) so now I can have some credit! The pineapple makes the cake really moist but make sure you chop it up fairly small first.

Cook 1¼ hours   Serves 12

6oz / 170g self-raising flour
8fl oz / 240ml vegetable oil
6oz / 170g caster sugar
2 eggs
8oz / 225g grated carrots
2oz / 55g chopped walnut pieces
8oz / 225g tinned pineapple chunks
1 teaspoon baking powder
½ teaspoon bicarbonate of soda
½ teaspoon cinnamon
½ teaspoon salt

Topping:
3oz / 85g cream cheese
6oz / 170g icing sugar
3oz / 85g soft butter
½ teaspoon vanilla essence
1oz / 25g chopped walnut pieces

1 Preheat the oven to 180°C / 350°F / gas mark 4
2 Whisk all the ingredients in the mixing bowl. Add the walnuts last.
3 Pour into a greased and lined 8 inch tin
4 Bake in the centre of the oven for 1¼ - 1½ hours or until golden brown
5 Turn out on to the wire rack to cool

For the topping:
1 Mix the cream cheese and soft butter
2 Gradually add the icing sugar and vanilla essence to the cream cheese and butter
3 Spread the topping over the cake and sprinkle with chopped walnuts

Everything changes meditation

Everything changes

Change can seem like a frightening prospect. In some ways, we want everything to remain the same – our relationships, our health, our emotions. In other ways, we fear change – relationships, health, emotions! Our thoughts are changing each second, in constant movement, sometimes feeling out of control. The reality is that at the smallest level, everything is in constant flux, forever moving and impermanent. This meditation helps us to embrace and welcome change as with this new understanding, we have the power to transform our lives.

The meditation

Take some time to settle into your chair or on your cushions. Allow your body to relax, letting go of any tensions you may notice. Let your eyes close. Allow your spine to lengthen in an upwards direction and your back to widen. Become aware of your feet taking up space on the ground beneath you. Rest your hands on your lap or cushion. Your breath is quiet and calm, and you are aware of the space and sounds around you. If thoughts arise, allow them to drift through your mind without becoming caught up or distracted by them.

Bring your attention to your body, beginning with your feet and working your way slowly through your legs, hips, belly, back, hands, arms, shoulders, neck and head. Notice the sensations in your body: the weight of your legs as you sit in the chair, the feel of the cushion under your hands, the movement of your breath in your chest, your heartbeat, the circulation of your blood. Contemplate for a few moments the changes going on right now, throughout your body.

At a deeper level, know that your cells are dying and being reborn every second, constantly changing to support your health and well-being. In your mind, thoughts, perceptions, judgements, ideas and inspirations move incessantly. Everything is changing. Stay with this thought for a few moments.

Expand your awareness outwards, into the space that surrounds you. All things that appear solid are vibrating and moving – your chair, the objects in the room, the building you live in, people, cars, the natural world – nothing is fixed. Have a strong sense of the nature of change. Through awareness of the transitory nature of all life, we can loosen our grip and begin to live. When we let go, we embrace without fear the essence of change.

Start to become aware of your feet beneath you, and your hands as they rest on your lap. Gradually notice the rest of your body: your legs, back, belly, arms, shoulders, neck and head. Extend your awareness to take in the space and sounds around you. Your mind is clear, bright and full of energy.

In your own time, bring your meditation to a close.

Things do not change;

we change

Henry David Thoreau

Christmas cake

At this time of year, we Airy Fairies have a Christmas gathering which means I get to try out different dishes and treats cooked by everyone else as they all bring food to share. This recipe has been generously donated by Janet, the Queen of Cakes, who has given me a very simple but delicious Christmas Cake recipe. It's just the job at this busy time of year. Thanks, Janet!

Note: If you want to ice the cake, spread some almond paste over it one week before icing.

Cook 1¾ hours   Serves 10 - 12

5oz / 140g soft margarine
5oz / 140g light Muscovado sugar
8oz / 225g self raising flour
2 eggs
6oz / 170g currants
2oz / 55g whole almonds, chopped
14oz / 400g jar luxury mincemeat

1 Preheat oven to 170°C / 325°F / gas mark 3

2 Grease and line the base and sides of an 8inch / 20cm deep round cake tin

3 Beat all the ingredients well for 1 minute in the mixing bowl until thoroughly mixed

4 Turn into the tin and level the surface

5 Bake in the centre of the oven for 1¾ hours or until the cake shrinks from the sides and test by inserting a skewer which should come out clean

6 Allow the cake to cool in the tin for 10 minutes before turning out to cool on a wire rack

Visit www.deborahcoote.com for details of workshops, events, Alexander Technique lessons, books and CDs, and how to set up your own meditation group.

The Alexander Technique is a method that helps you to recognise and release unwanted physical and mental tension through increased awareness of the self. It can raise a person's consciousness so that life becomes happier, healthier and more fulfilling. For a list of Alexander Technique teachers, visit **www.stat.org**

The semi-supine position allows for optimum rest for the mind and body. This will help you to recognise and release muscular tension, and cultivate stillness. Lay on the floor with your knees bent and a book underneath your head, placing your hands on your abdomen. When you get up, you can try to maintain this awareness of yourself as you go about your daily activities.

The power of group meditation on crime, as well as health and well being, has been written about by various people, so have a browse on the net to find out more. Lynn McTaggert's book, *The Intention Experiment*, brings together some recent and important scientific studies on this subject. Also, *The Global Consciousness Project* is well worth visiting on the internet.

Books
There are too many to mention individually but here are a few:

Teach Yourself to Meditate by Eric Harrison is a really useful and practical book.

For the more spiritual try *The Miracle of Mindfulness* by Thich Nhat Hanh, *Stillness Speaks* by Eckhart Tolle and *Zen Mind, Beginner's Mind* by Susuki Roshi.

For **Tibetan singing bowls** visit **www.handcrafted.uk.com**   Tel 01363 772974

Index